Ray Greene Huling

The Rhode Island Emigration to Nova Scotia

Ray Greene Huling

The Rhode Island Emigration to Nova Scotia

ISBN/EAN: 9783337379612

Printed in Europe, USA, Canada, Australia, Japan

Cover: Foto ©ninafisch / pixelio.de

More available books at **www.hansebooks.com**

Rhod Emigration

otia.

.

g, A. M.,
Mass.

ce, R. I.,
Reprinted from the Narragansett Historical Register,
April, 1889.

THE RHODE ISLAND EMIGRATION TO NOVA SCOTIA.

By Ray Greene Huling, A. M., New Bedford, Mass.

RHODE ISLANDERS emigrating to Nova Scotia? How is that? We are not unacquainted with migrations from our little state, – all too small from the outset to contain the adventurous spirit of her sons. Now they carry our well known names to spread over Long Island and the Jerseys. Again, they colonize the western hills of the Bay State, and move northward to the Green Mountains. Then they flock to the banks of the Hudson and the ill-fated valley of Wyoming. Central New York abounds with their descendants, and of the later waves of migration to the remoter states and the Pacific slope there is no need to speak. " Westward the star of empire takes its way," says Bancroft, and the Rhode Islander seems ever to have had his eye upon that luminary.

But when did a colony turn eastward to Nova Scotia? Ah yes! They must have been a group of Tories, paying by exile and loss of estates the penalty for adherence to King George in the terrible days of the Revolution. Some such there were from the southern counties of the state, it is true, but I cannot learn that they united in any settlement in Nova Scotia.

No! The colony of which I speak left the parent stock when all were alike loyal to the sovereign of Great Britain, — indeed at just the juncture when it was the proudest boast of every New Englander that he was a British subject. For there were almost then sounding on the air the cannon which announced the fall of the *fleur-de-lis* over all America and the universal rule upon this western land of English law and Saxon civilization. These colonists went out not by compulsion but by free choice, and indeed upon an urgent invitation. Their aim was simply to open new homes, as had their fathers, in a new land and on richer soil.

One of the saddest episodes in the long struggle for supremacy between the French and the English on this continent was the expatriation of the Acadians. Longfellow in his Evangeline has told us, with a poet's license, all the melancholy story, — and even more. Our historical reading has, no doubt, explained the sad necessity of the step as a military precaution, but the pictures limned by the poet grow even brighter as our eyes rest upon the scenes described.

" This is the forest primeval. The murmuring pines and
        the hemlocks,
Bearded with moss, and in garments green, indistinct in
        the twilight,
Stand like the Druids of eld, with voices sad and prophetic,
Stand like harpers hoar, with beards that rest on their
        bosoms.

Loud from his rocky caverns, the deep voiced neighboring
    ocean,
Speaks, and in accents disconsolate answers the wails of
    the forest.
           *   *   *   *   *   *   *   *
In the Acadian land, on the shores of the Basin of Minas,
Distant, secluded, still, the little village of Grand-Pre
Lay in the fruitful valley. Vast meadows stretched to the
    eastward,
Giving the village its name, and pasture to flocks without
'   number.
Dikes, that the hands of the farmers had raised with labors
    incessant,
Shut out the turbulent tides; but at stated seasons the
    flood-gates
Opened, and welcomed the sea to wander at will o'er the
    meadows.
West and south there were fields of flax, and orchards and
    cornfields
Spreading afar and unfenced o'er the plain; and away to
    the northward
Blomidon rose, and the forests old; and aloft on the moun-
    tains
Sea fogs pitched their tents, and mists from the mighty
    Atlantic
Looked on the happy valley, but ne'er from their station
    descended."

Such pictures as these it was that attracted to Acadia, within five years after the expulsion of the French inhabitants,
the nucleus of the colony from Rhode Island, of which this
paper treats.

The country comprising the Maritime Provinces was in the hands of the French and the English by turns until the year 1713, when by the Peace of Utrecht Acadia was ceded by France to Great Britain, in whose possession it has ever since remained. For many years later, however, the only English in the district were the troops at the various posts scattered over the country and a few civilians connected with the government, and with the supply of the army. The inhabitants of Nova Scotia were chiefly French farmers and fishermen, living mainly about the Minas Basin and on the Annapolis River. Over these the English government maintained but a feeble control. In 1749 the English themselves laid the foundation for a settlement on the beautiful and capacious harbor of Chebucto and named it Halifax. A jealousy soon sprang up between these English settlers and their French neighbors, the nearest of whom were at Pisiquid, now Windsor, some forty-five miles away. Soon war was renewed between the English and the French Governments, during which both the Acadian settlers and the Indians in Nova Scotia, though professedly neutral, were found in ardent sympathy with the enemy. Blood and religion were stronger than political relations. The Acadians repeatedly refused to take the oath of allegiance to the British Crown, except one so modified as to exclude service against the French. Moreover, the restless young spirits among them, either openly or in disguise, were found engaged with the Canadians and Indians in forays against the English. The English Governor, Charles Lawrence, clearly saw that the Acadian settlements on the Annapolis and the Basin of Minas offered a constant rendezvous for attack upon the feeble settlement of Halifax, and determined upon the forcible removal of the French to the southern colonies, with such dispersion of them as would effectually prevent their concerted return. To accomplish this required hasty and secret preparations. No word was sent even to the Home Government though the two Admirals on the station were consulted. Seizing an opportune moment when a New England force under Lieut. Col. John Winslow was at hand, brought thither for the capture of the French forts at the head of the Bay of Fundy, Governor Lawrence instructed his officers to collect the Acadians in the whole region , prevent any from escaping and put all on board transports which would be provided. Families were to be kept together as far as possible. The work was done by Winslow at Grand-Pre and that neighborhood, and by Capt. Murray at Pisiquid. The blow fell early in September 1755, and was made by the New England troops as light as their orders permitted. After a little waiting, in order to bring in the men who had fled to the woods, the vessels sailed bearing three thousand souls from home and native land to various points along the coast in what is now the United States. To preclude a return the houses about Grand-Pre, certainly, were burned, but elsewhere the work seems to have been less complete.

The government at Halifax had now its will. The mass of the Acadian settlers had been driven from their homes, the houses and barns had been fired, and the stock slaughtered or left to become wild. The scattered remnant of the farmers and fishermen were hiding in the woods, or had hurried to the Indian camps, or else had taken refuge with the French upon the St. Lawrence. The rich dike lands lay without care, the orchards were of no use to man, the uplands bore no crops. Some of the fairest spots Nature had planted upon the Atlantic, rendered fairer by the improvements of man for more than a century, were now relapsing to wilderness because of neglect. Settlers, therefore, were earnestly looked for, – settlers whose allegiance should be undoubted, and whose right arms might ever be ready for service in the wars of Britain.

The Home Government desired that the vacant lands should be distributed among disbanded soldiers, but Governor Lawrence strenuously opposed this. A soldier himself, he maintained that no class of persons was by previous training so unfitted to become the founders of a new country as soldiers. Every soldier who had come to Halifax, he added from his personal observation, had either returned to England or become a dramseller. The new settlers must be men of a different type.

To this sensible remonstrance the Lords of Trade acceded. Governor Lawrence was left free to pursue his own plans for the peopling of the despoiled farms. With excellent judgement the Governor turned for help to the stout-hearted colonists at the southwest, by whose valor and perseverance so much of the work of winning new France for the British Crown had been accomplished. A proclamation was adopted in Council Oct. 12, 1758, relating to the settlement of the vacated French lands. Printed descriptions were circulated in which the advantages of the soil were highly praised.

The Governor announced that he was ready to receive proposals for the settlement of this region, containing " one hundred thousand acres of intervale plow lands, producing wheat, rye, barley, oats, hemp, flax, etc., which have been cultivated for than a hundred years past and never fail of crops nor need manuring. Also more than one hundred thousand acres of upland, cleared and stocked with English grass, planted with orchards, gardens etc. These lands with good husbandry produce often two loads of hay to the acre. The wild and unimproved lands adjoining to the above are well timbered and wooded with beech, black birch, ash, oak,

pine, fir etc. All these lands are so intermixed that every
single farmer may have a proportionate quantity of plow land
grass land and wood land, and all are situated about the Bay
of Fundi upon rivers navigable for ships of burthen."

Throughout New England, and especially south-eastern
New England, this flattering proclamation excited great interest. There were enough old soldiers of the French Wars,
who had seen service at Louisburg and Fort Cumberland, or
had been the agents in expelling the Acadian farmers, to
confirm by word of mouth the accuracy of the statements
made in the proclamation. Consequently the Nova Scotian
agent at Boston, Thomas Hancock, (the uncle of John Hancock of Revolutionary fame), then the richest and most influential merchant of the town, soon had several propositions
to submit to Governor Lawrence. There were numerous settlers ready to come, but as the proclamation had been silent
on all points except the quality of the land, his Excellency
was required to state in explicit terms, the nature of the constitution, the protection to be afforded to the civil and religious liberties of the subject, and the extent of the elective
franchise of the people. There had been too much of stern
conflict upon these points by the people of New England for
such considerations to be ignored.

Their answer was soon ready for them. Jan. 11, 1759,
Governor Lawrence sent forth from the Council Chamber at
Halifax, a second proclamation, – a most important state paper, which, as it contains the solemn assurance of the Government on the points named above, has been not inaptly
styled, says Judge Haliburton, the Charter of Nova Scotia.
It is worth quoting in full.

        2

" By his Excellency Charles Lawrence, Esq., Captain General and Governor-in-chief, in and over his Majesty's Province of Nova Scotia, or Acadia, in America, Vice Admiral of the same, etc., etc.

" Whereas since the issuing of the proclamation dated the 12th., day of Oct. 1758, relative to settling the vacant lands in this Province, I have been informed by Thomas Hancock, Esq., Agent for the affairs of Nova Scotia, at Boston, that sundry applications have been made to him in consequence thereof, by persons who are desirous of settling the said lands, and of knowing what particular encouragement the Government will give them, whether any allowance of provisions will be given at their first settlement, what quantity of land will be given to each person, what quit rents they are to pay, what the constitution of the Government is, whether any, and what taxes are to be paid, and whether they will be allowed the free exercise of their religion? I have therefore thought fit, with the advice of his Majesty's Council, to issue this proclamation, hereby declaring, in answer to the said enquiries, that by his Majesty's Royal instructions, I am empowered to make grants on the following proportions:

That townships are to consist of one hundred thousand acres of land, that they do include the best and most profitable land, and also that they do comprehend such rivers as may be at or near such settlement and to extend as far up into the Country as conveniently may be, taking in a necessary part of the sea-coast. That the quantities of land granted will be in proportion to the abilities of the planter to settle, cultivate, and enclose the same. That one hundred acres of wild wood land will be allowed to every person, being master or mistress of a family, for himself or herself, and fifty acres for every white or black man, woman, or child, of which such person's family shall consist at the actual time of making the grant, subject to the payment of a quit rent of one shilling sterling per annum for every fifty acres; such quit rent to commence at the expiration of ten years from the date of each grant, and to be paid for his Majesty's use to his Receiver General, at Halifax, or to his Deputy on the spot.

" That the grantees will be obliged by their said grants to plant, cultivate, improve, or enclose, one third part of their lands within the space of ten years, another third part within the space of twenty years and the remaining third part within the space of thirty years, from the date of their grants. That no one person can possess more than one thousand acres by grant, on his or their own name.

" That every grantee, upon giving proof that he or she has fulfilled the terms and conditions of his or her grants, shall be entitled to another grant in the proportion and upon the conditions above mentioned. That the Government of Nova Scotia is constituted like those of the neighbouring Colonies; the Legislature consisting of a Governor, Council, and House of Assembly, and every township, as soon as it shall consist of fifty families, will be entitled to send two Representatives to the General Assembly. The Courts of Justice are also constituted in like manner with those of the Massachusetts, Connecticut, and other Northern Colonies. That as to the article of religion full liberty of conscience, both of his Majesty's royal instructions and a late act of the General Assembly of this Province, is secured to persons of all persuasions, Papists excepted, as may more fully appear by the following abstract of the said act, viz : —

' Protestants dissenting from the Church of England, whether they be Calvinists, Lutherans, Quakers, or under what denomination soever, shall have free liberty of conscience, and may erect and build Meeting Houses for public worship, and may choose and elect Ministers for the carrying on divine service, and administration of the sacrament, according to their several opinions, and all contracts made between their Ministers and congregations for the support of their Ministry, are hereby declared valid, and shall have their full force and effect according to the tenor and conditions thereof, and all such Dissenters shall be excused from any rates or taxes to be made or levied for the support of the Established Church of England.'

" That no taxes have hitherto been laid upon his Majesty's subjects within this Province, nor are there any fees of office taken upon issuing the grants of land.

" That I am not authorized to issue any bounty of provisions; and I do hereby declare that I am ready to lay out the lands and make grants immediately under the conditions above described, and to receive and transmit to the Lords Commissioners for Trade and Plantations, in order that the same may be laid before his Majesty for approbation, such further proposals as may be offered by any body of people, for settling an entire township under other conditions that they may conceive more advantages to the undertakers.

" That forts are established in the neighborhood of the lands proposed to be settled, and are garrisoned by his Majesty's troops, with a view of giving all manner of aid and protection to the settlers, if hereafter there should be need.

Given in the Council Chamber at Halifax, this 11th., day of January, 1759, in the 32nd· year of His Majesty's reign.

(Signed.)   CHARLES LAWRENCE. "

The significance of this document in one respect must have struck the attention of all who are Rhode Islanders in spirit; I refer to its lofty sentiments with regard to liberty of conscience. The inhabitants of Nova Scotia in succeeding periods have had reason to be grateful to these colonists of 1760 for having elicited such satisfactory pledges from the royal government that no abridgement of their religious priviliges should be suffered in consequence of their removal. And Governor Lawrence himself builded better than he knew when he gave his sanction to measures so liberal. The single exception to complete religious toleration, – in the case of the Roman Catholics, – was never, so far as I can learn, made practically grievous to any individuals. Certainly there have always been French Catholics within the province and considerable emigrations of Scotch and Irish Catholics have at times been encouraged. The spirit of the community has been tuned to a key even higher than the letter of their ancient law.

The proclamation of Governor Lawrence was favorably received in New England, and led to active steps toward emigration. In April, 1759, agents from a number of persons in Connecticut and Rhode Island who designed to become settlers on the Bay of Fundy came to Halifax. They were Major Robert Dennison and Messrs. Jonathan Harris, Joseph Otis and James Fuller from Connecticut, and Mr. John Hicks from Rhode Island. A Council was held at the house of Governor Lawrence at which these gentlemen were in attendance. They put several questions to the board respecting the terms of the proposed grants, and received very encouraging answers.

As they were the first applicants they were promised some aid from government for the poorer families. The vessels belonging to the Province were to be at the service of the settlers to bring them with their stock and furniture to Nova Scotia. Arms were to be supplied for a small number and protection by block houses and garrisons. Furthermore the government expressly engaged that the settlers should not be subjected to impressment.

The agents were highly pleased with the results of the conference and desired to be shown the lands upon which settlement was proposed. They were sent to the Basin of Minas on the armed scow Halifax, attended by Charles Morris, a member of the Council and Chief Land Surveyor of the Province. An officer of artillery with eight soldiers served as guard for the party.

In May the agents returned to Halifax, after having viewed the vacant lands from which the French farmers had so rudely been torn. So well satisfied were they with their inspection that immediate arrangements were made to secure the grants of land. The four gentlemen from Connecticut who represented 330 signers to an agreement for settlement, proposed to take up a township adjoining the river Gaspereaux including the great marshes, the Grand Pre of Longfellow's story, and constituting the present township of Horton. This township of 100.000 acres was to be given in fee simple, subject to the proposed quit-rent, to 200 families. Block-houses were were to be built and garrisoned for their defence. Fifty families of the number were to have from government an allowance of one bushel of corn to each person per month or an equivalent in other grain. This was to continue for one year. These families were also furnished arms and ammunition for defence. All the people with their movables, stock, etc., were to be transported at the expense of the government.

There was also made an agreement for 150 families to settle 100.000 acres on the river Canard to the westward upon the same terms. This township was named Cornwallis. Formal grants of Horton and Cornwallis passed the seal of the Province on May 21. 1759.

At the same time Mr. John Hicks from Rhode Island, and a Mr. Amos Fuller (possibly the James Fuller of Connecticut named above, though Murdoch gives the name Amos) desired the Governor and Council to reserve land for them and their constituents at Pisiquid on the north side of the river. (So says Murdoch. The settlement was made upon the west side also.) They engaged to settle fifty families in 1759 and fifty more in 1760 on the same terms as were accorded to Horton and Cornwallis. This was agreed to, and July 21, 1759 a formal grant was made of 50.000 acres between the river Pisiquid and the town of Horton. Of this tract a long range of mountains forms the rear, a gradually sloping upland the centre, and a border of marsh the front. To this township the name Falmouth was given, and here was the home of a part of the first settlers from Rhode Island.

That summer of 1759 was not a season of entire peace in Nova Scotia. During this very month of July a party of French and Indians, about a hundred in number, appeared before Fort Edward at Pisiquid and continued there some days, but departed without an engagement. The same month a party of committee men inspecting lands near Cape Sable was fired upon by the same or a similar band of foes. Three fishing vessels were captured off Canso by the Acadian French. Even across the harbor from Halifax and within sight of the citadel, two persons had been murdered, while numbers of the enemy had been seen lurking about Lunenburg and Fort Sackville. In view of these facts the Government postponed the new settlements along the Basin of Minas to the following spring. But additional settlements, chiefly by men from Massachusetts, were projected at Chignecto and Cobequid in the north, and at Granville and Annapolis in the south of the province.

The succeeding autumn brought to Governor Lawrence and to New England the joyful tidings of the fall of Quebec, though their joy was shadowed by the death of the gallant Wolfe at the very moment of victory. The French were not yet wholly vanquished, it is true, but had retired upon Montreal. Yet their influence along the lower St. Lawrence and in the Maritime Provinces was nearly gone. Within eighteen months thereafter, there was concluded at Halifax a solemn treaty of peace with the leading chiefs of the Micmacs, by which they transferred their allegiance from France to England, and ceased to be an annoyance to the province.

The first settlers from Rhode Island arrived in the spring of 1760. Haliburton says there arrived from Rhode Island four schooners carrying one hundred settlers. I am inclined to think, however, that the earliest to arrive were the persons referred to in the following document.

" List of Settlers brought from Newport Rhode Island to Falmouth Nov. in the Sloop Sally. Jona. Lovatt, Master, in May, 1760.

		Persons	
Benjamin Sanford & family		7	£ 8, 15, 0
Nathaniel Reynolds,	do.	4	5. 0, 0
Samuel Bentley,	do.	2	2. 10. 0
James Hervie,	do.	5	6. 5, 0
James Smith,	do.	6	7, 10, 0
John Chambers,	do.	1	1, 5. 0
James Weeden,	do.	6	7, 10, 0

Joshua Sanford,	do.	3	3, 15, 0
John Hervie,	do.	1	1, 5, 0

In the whole   35 persons

35 persons at £1, 5, 0., each is £43, 15, 0.

These are to Certify that the above is a true and perfect list of the settlers brought to the township of Falmouth in the Sloop Sally and of the numbers of their families as appears by the   of the several persons therein named.

(No signature.)

List of settlers brought from Newport in Rhode Island to Falmouth in the Sloop Lydia, Saml Toby Master, in May, 176).

Benjamin Burdin & family	3	persons.	
Caleb Lake	do	7	"
Henry Tucker	do.	3	"
Jams Mosher	do.	8	"

23 persons at £1, 5, 0 each is £28, 15, 0 "

(The above copy was kindly made for me by Thomas B. Akins Esq., of Halifax.)

This document is in the handwriting of Isaac Deschamps, then Government Agent and Magistrate at Fort Edward, across the river from the Rhode Island settlements. He was ever a firm friend of the Rhode Islanders and often represented them in the Provincial Assembly. Subsequently he rose to the dignity of Chief Justice of the Supreme Court of the Province. The paper is evidently a memorandum of the bills presented by the masters of the vessels for services in transporting the immigrants. An extended search has thus far failed to bring to light other similar lists, which must have existed.   4

The names, except that of Chambers, will readily be recognized as common family names in the Island towns of our state and the mainland towns near by. Indeed the same is true of a large proportion of the names of persons to whom lots were granted in the townships of Falmouth and Newport. Lists of these are subjoined in an appendix. They purport to have been made in the first year of settlement, but undoubtedly contain names added subsequently as new settlers arrived.

On arrival the Rhode Island men separated into two settlements, one on the north side of the Pisiquid and St. Croix, and the other on the west side of the former river. For a year both settlements were called Falmouth, one being termed East Falmouth, and the other West Falmouth. First let us follow the fortunes of the latter, which finally had the original name all to itself.

The first proprietors' meeting was held June 10, 1760. The location is stlyed " Falmouth on the west side of the Pisiquid river." The chairman was Shubael Dimock, a Baptist from Mansfield, Connecticut, who, finding himself uncomfortable at home by reason of his religious belief, had joined the Rhode Islanders. (He afterwards went to reside at Newport, N. S., where he died in 1781 at the age of 73.) The clerk was Abner Hall. Three committee-men were chosen to manage affairs : Wignal Cole, Abner Hall, and David Randall. At the outset 200 acres were laid out for a common, 60 acres for a town, (i. e. a village), and a certain tract for a public cemetery. Each man had a half-acre town lot, a six-acre lot, a ten-acre marsh lot, a farm lot, and two wood lots. One of these was from 100 to 200 acres in size quite accessible, the other contained about 400 acres back on Horton Mountain.

The settlement grew steadily although not with the rapidity of the more open and level towns of Horton and Cornwallis. In the early autumn after their arrival, the settlers learned of the capitulation of the French forces at Montreal, by which all prospect of further war was prevented. It was late in the season, however, when the farmers had come, and the crops for the first year were scanty. Yet by the opening of winter, the President of the Council could write to the Board of Trade at London thus:

" I have the satisfaction to acquaint your Lordships that the townships of Horton, Cornwallis, and Falmouth are so well established that everything bears a hopeful appearance; as soon as these townships were laid out by the Surveyor, palesaded (sic) forts were erected in each of them by order of the late Governor with room to secure all the inhabitants, who were formed into a militia to join what troops could be spared to oppose any attempts that might be formed against them by Indian tribes, which had not then surrendered, and bodies of French inhabitants who were hovering about the country. After the necessary business, the proper season coming on they were employed in gathering hay for the winter. One thousand tons were provided for Horton, five hundred for Cornwallis, and six hundred for Falmouth, and about this time they put some corn and roots into the ground, and began to build their houses."

(Charles Lawrence, by whose wisdom and kind services the New Englanders had been induced to come to Nova Scotia, had died suddenly in October, 1760, before he had seen the full fruition of his generous plans.)

In Falmouth the upland was in very good condition for planting and was much more extensive than the marsh. The dike-lands were at this time in very poor condition. In 1755

the dikes had been cut in some places to discourage the return
of the Acadians, but the most serious harm had been done
by an extraordinary storm in November 1759, which had
made breaches in nearly all the dikes, and overflowed the
drained marshes with salt tides five feet higher than were ever
seen there before. Governor Lawrence had begun repairs
before his death, and the work was continued by his successor.
Subsequently vastly larger areas were reclaimed by the English than the French had ever tried to drain.

Fortunately we have the means of looking upon the physical
features of Falmouth with much the same vision as that of
the early settlers. Under date of Jan. 9, 1762, Charles
Morris, the Chief Surveyor previously mentioned, made to
the Government an extended report upon the condition of the
various townships of the province. Here is what he says
about Falmouth. (Mss. in Province Library at Halifax.)

" This township was granted to one hundred proprietors,
of which eighty families are at present settled, containing
350 persons. The settlement was begun in 1760. Several
other grants of the lands adjoining have been granted and
added to this township, so that the whole will consist of one
hundred and fifty proprietors or shares This township contains about 2500 acres of marsh land. [Judge Haliburton
says 1184 acres of diked marsh in 1828.] and 3,000 acres
of cleared upland, the proprietors having divided the cleared
land and improvable land into lots. It amounts to about
eighty acres to each share. The other parts of the township
being the termination of two long ranges of mountains is
broken mountain and steep precipices and mostly unimprova-
ble lands. These inhabitants have imported large quantities
of cattle and have this year cut hay sufficient for supporting
them, but the excessive drought of the summer has blasted

most of their corn. The river Pisiquid running through this town is navigable for sloops to all the settlements, there being three fathom at high water for six miles. The town is situated in the centre of the settlements. The woods having suffered at the same time as Horton, the growth of timber is small, of the same kind as Horton."

In another place he explains this last allusion as follows: " In Horton the natural growth is spruce, fir, white birch, poplar and white pine. The growth of timber is small, the woods having been levelled by fire about fifty years since."

The river Pisiquid, now called the Avon, as it flows out between Falmouth and Windsor, receives the St. Croix. By the union is formed a broad basin some two miles wide, across which at low tide men have been known to wade, but which at high tide contains from fifty to sixty feet of reddish muddy water, having during the flood a current inward strong enough to bear " three-masters " up stream. To the northward of this basin a part of the Rhode Island men had chosen their farms including the thirteen families who came in the sloops Sally and Lydia. Their first landing place, now called Avondale, is a flourishing ship-building village, abounding in Rhode Island names. As we have said, the settlement was first called East Falmouth, but in 1761 it received with the formal grant of the township, a new name, Newport, which it still retains. The tradition prevails that this name was given in honor of the old home of the settlers in Rhode Island, but this explanation, though so natural, is certainly incorrect, as is shown by the following letter.

(For a copy of this letter, I am indebted to David Allison, LL. D. Superintendent of Education for Nova Scotia, a native of Newport, from whom numerous courtesies have been received.)

Halifax, March 31, 1761.

Sir:

Capt. Maloney, upon the application of the Inhabitants of Horton and Cornwallis, is to return to New London to take in provisions, but half his lading. He is then to proceed to Newport to take in provision for East and West Falmouth. He has orders to take Dr. Ellis and family and effects and one Mr. Mather, [this name is somewhat uncertain], if they are ready.

The Inhabitants of East Falmouth have petitioned to be set off as a distinct town and it has been mentioned in Council, but nothing conclusive done. There is an objection because of the fewness of proprietors, but if they will consent to have an addition of 20 rights, a sufficient quantity of land being added to that end, I believe they may obtain it. I have proposed to have it named Newport, from my Lord Newport, a friend of Mr. Belcher's, and which I believe will be agreeable to the people if they think it will be of advantage to them. I think the addition of 20 shares will be no disadvantage, as they have land equivalent. You can inform yourself of their opinion on this head.

I shall endeavor to send the iron by the vessel bringing the provision.

I am obliged to you for the assistance you gave my son among the inhabitants.

It will not be long before you will be here and then I will fully inform you of the other affairs, till when I am, in haste,

Sir, your most obt servant,

C. Morris,

(Surveyor General)

To Isaac Deschamps, Esq.

Fort Edward.

This same gentleman in the report of Jan. 9, 1762, previously mentioned, gives a description of the 58,000 acres to which the name Newport was affixed:

" This township, granted to seventy proprietors, began its settlement in 1761. (He must refer to the grant of 1761. The settlement began previous to June 1760.) The present number of families is sixty, containing about 240 persons. They imported a sufficient number of neat cattle and have this summer cut hay sufficient for them. They have also raised a considerable quantity of English grain, but not enough to subsist them, being cut short by the drought. They have but little improved land in proportion to the other townships. It contains about 1,000 acres of marsh land and 600 acres of cleared lands. This township contains in proportion to its bigness a greater quantity of improvable lands than any of the fore-mentioned townships. The soil in general is rich and great part free from stones; it is heavy timbered, not having suffered by fire, as the others neighboring. Its natural growth is fir, pine, spruce, oak, beach, (sic) birch, etc. The river Conetcook runs through the middle of this township, navigable for sloops at high water for ten miles, and on the southern end the river St. Croix, navigable for four miles."

The names of the grantees of Newport are given in the appendix. Among them are a dozen or more which are plainly not of Rhode Island origin. It will be remembered that Mr. Morris spoke in his letter of " an addition of 20 rights " to the original settlement. The great mass of the names, however, are the same as are well known now in the southern counties of our state. Perhaps the most interesting single name is that of " William Hallyburton," for he was the great-grandfather of Judge Thomas C. Haliburton, the

distinguished Nova Scotian historian and humorist, better
known as "Sam Slick."

[Since it is not generally known that this family is of
Rhode Island origin, let me here insert a copy of a certificate
now existing in Newport, R. I., which is conclusive on this
point.

" Newport, Rhode Island, }
September 15th, 1762. }

This may Certify all it may Concern that I the Subscrib-
er did sometime in the Fall of the year 1760 draw a memorandum (for Mrs. Sarah Wright late deceased) of several
Bequests, &c., which she was minded to make, But any of
the Particulars I do not really Remember.

William Hallyburton.

I further add, the said Memorandum was drawn at the Re-
quest and Desire of the said Sarah Wright.

Newport }
to wit. }   Newport,
                  Sept. 15th day, A. D. 1762.

Personally appeared the above-named William
Hallyburton and made Solemn Oath to the Truth of the above
said Evidence and Signed the same.

Taken and Sworn to the Day and Date above said.

Before me,   John Davis Jr.,
Justice of the Peace."

It is interesting in this connection to note that among
those who removed to Halifax from Newport, R. I., at the
close of the Revolution, was a Dr. John Haliburton, father
of the late Sir Brenton Haliburton, Chief Justice of Nova
Scotia at his death in 1865.]

The records of Newport, still extant, show the same pro-
cedure in general as on the other side of the river. The proprietors held their first meeting on June 9, 1760, one day

earlier than at Falmouth proper. James Weeden was chosen moderator and Zerobabel Waistcoat clerk. Captain Edward York, Joseph Baley and Benjamin Sanford were chosen a committee to regulate affairs. A month later they ran out "town lots," providing for a compact village at what is now Avondale. Subsequently other villages have sprung up, but none of large size. The neighboring town of Windsor, clustering about Fort Edward, became the business centre for Newport and Falmouth, as well as for its own township. The settlers at Newport, as also at Falmouth, made provision for a school, and for religion, in their division of lands. Each proprietor appears to have had by allotment some 500 acres, partly marsh, partly upland, and largely woodland, besides six acres in the proposed "town." Much of this land, however, was not improved for many years.

The township has had a quiet and peaceful development as a farming region, with some ship building and some quarrying of "plaster." Being the nearest fertile district to Halifax, it has always had a ready market for such products as were needed by a garrison town, especially for horses and hay. The marsh lands are apparently of inexhaustible fertility and the uplands of good quality. To the settlers of Rhode Island origin have been added numerous others of English, Scotch, and Scotch-Irish descent, all a worthy stock for the upbuilding of a new country. The names of Mosher, Simpson, Smith, Sanford, and Knowles are still common and prominent. The faces to be seen on the hillsides are the exact counterparts of those in our own rural districts. Indeed in riding over the pleasant hills of both Newport and Falmouth, everything reminded me of certain parts of my native state, except the beds of the rivers. For here we have nothing like the Avon, the ancient Pisiquid, at low tide, a broad

4

slimy chasm, forty to fifty feet deep, lined everywhere with a reddish ooze. It was when gazing on this spectacle from Windsor, that Charles Dudley Warner declared that he never understood before how much water added to a river.

There is still a third township on the Bay of Fundy which had its origin in a colony from Rhode Island, but of this I cannot speak at length. It is the town of Sackville in New Brunswick, lying on a part of the famous Tantemar marshes, " the granary of Nova Scotia." Some twenty five families had settled there in the summer of 1761 and the other grantees were expected by Mr Morris to arrive in the spring of 1762, as many of them had been down the previous year to build houses in preparation for their families. There is at Halifax in the Province Libary a " List of the Sub- scribers for the Township lying on the Tantemar River, Represented by Benjamin Thurber, Cyprian Sterry, and Edmund Jenckes from Providence in Rhodisland," which list is given in the appendix. The 154 names upon it are nearly all common in the northern towns of Rhode Island. Probably most of them represent actual settlers, who were at Sackville for a time, if not permanently. For the settlement at this point had a somewhat different history from those of which we have spoken. There was, for instance, a whole Baptist Church in Swansea, Massachusetts, that emigrated bodily, under the leadership of the pastor, Nathan Mason, to Sackville in 1763 and after a residence there of eight years returned to its former abode. Moreover, when the War for Independence broke out, many of the settlers at Sackville and Cumberland sympathized so strongly with their brethren in the revolting colonies, that they joined the patriots in arms, and in consequence lost their homes, as the Province re- mained loyal to King George. Yet, I am told, the majority of the population of the township today is of New England ancestry. As I rode through Sackville upon the train, I got a glimse of Mt. Allison University, and Mt. Allison Ladies' College, institutions for higher education, which give some hint of the prosperity of the township and of the type of character prevailing among its residents. Rhode Island has no reason to be ashamed of her representatives at the head of the Bay of Fundy.

Of individual reminiscences relating to the period of the immigration of 1760, little can now be obtained. Not many of that first generation became prominent above their fellows in matters that have interest for succeeding generations. There was, indeed, but one of the Rhode Island settlers whom I should care to follow personally in this paper, and in that one I hope to find you sharing a hearty interest.

His name was Henry Alline. (As to spelling, the name is variously written Alline, Allin, and Allen.) Although he died of consumption at the early age of 36 years, he had meantime revolutionized the religious condition of his adopted land and had cleared the way for men of a different type to build strong and sure. Indeed his services had earned for him the title of the Whitefield of Nova Scotia.

Henry Alline was born in Newport, R. I., June 14, 1748. His father and mother, William and Rebecca Alline, appear not to have been of the Rhode Island family of similar name, but by their son are said to have been born and brought up in Boston, where he had numerous relatives. The boy Henry was but twelve years old on that summer in 1760 when with his father's family he clambered over the sloop's side and landed in the red mud of the Pisiquid at Falmouth. In his journal, marvellously constructed in a short-hand that is well nigh a cipher, he has told us how his boyish fears were stirred by the frequent rumors that the Indians were about rising, and by the occasional coming of the Micmacs themselves, with their faces made hideous by war paint, to declare that the English should not settle in their country.

At an early age he became the subject of very strong religious impressions. Fear of death and the judgement constantly haunted him. Yet for twenty years he lived a miserable life under the terrors of the law and the lash of an accusing conscience, but stubborn and unyielding. In his twenty-seventh year for the first time he obtained light and learned to hope in Christ. Through the prayerful study of the bible, and the reading of religious books, he then obtained more correct views of his own character, and the disposition of God to save repentant sinners. When finally enabled to rest firmly upon the atonement of Jesus Christ, his joy in the possession of pardon became as intense as his depression under a sense of guilt had previously been. " Oh! the astonishing wonders of His grace," he exclaimed, " and the ocean of redeeming love. Millions and millions of praise to His name! And oh! the unspeakable wisdom and beauty of the glorious plan of life and salvation." The emotional type of his religious life, so evident in these quotations, was never changed. It was the key at once to the extent and the character of his whole work.

At this time he attempted to take passage for New England in order to secure the education necessary to enable him to preach the gospel. It was, however, at the outbreak of the Revolution, and communication was not easy. He returned to Falmouth and soon commenced to address his friends and neighbors. For three years he preached almost daily, confining his meetings to the neighboring townships, and meeting with much hardship and opposition. In 1779 he was regularly ordained, and thereafter roamed through the length and breadth of the lower provinces, on horseback in summer and on snowshoes in winter, visiting every English speaking settlement, and everywhere arousing intense excitement, which took practical form in breaking up old church establishments and forming new societies. In August 1783, he found himself doomed for the grave, and started upon a journey to New England and a milder climate. On the way he preached as opportunity offered, but was overtaken by the destroyer while still in New Hampshire, and died at North Hampton in that state Feb. 2, 1784, without having reached the longed for refuge with relatives at Boston. His young life seemed fairly to have burned out with the intensity of its own fires.

Henry Alline was not an educated man; nor yet was he illiterate, for from the age of nine he was a devoted reader of thoughtful books. His journal shows evidence of great intellectual activity, and, indeed, of marked natural gifts for the pursuit of philosophy. Yet he was too fully absorbed in his religious work to devote much time to study or to literary composition. The most important of his literary productions are two books published after his death. The one is " *Hymns and Spiritual Songs*," a collection of nearly five hundred original hymns, which had reached a third edition in 1797. The other is his " *Life and Journal*," published at Boston in 1806. Both display genuine power, but need to be judged by the standard of his day, rather than by the criteria of our own highly favored age.

The first effect of Alline's religious efforts certainly appeared to be more largely for evil than for good. He broke in upon the settled congregations of the day with a deter-

mined purpose to disturb the existing ecclesiastical relations
and this purpose was accomplished, even to painful results.
Families were divided ; old neighbors became fierce enemies;
old churches became disintegrated, and new organizations
took their places.

But there were reasons why such pioneer work in religion
was needed. The churches of the provinces were then apparently at a very low ebb spiritually. If we may believe
John Wesley, the clergymen of the Church of England in
this region were not all worthy of their appointment. In
1780 that divine wrote to the Bishop of London as follows :

" Your Lordship observes there are three ministers in that
country (Newfoundland) already. True, my lord; but
what are three to watch over the souls in that extensive country. Suppose there were three score of such missionaries in
the country ; could I in conscience recommend these souls to
their care ? Do they take care of their own souls ? If they
do, (I speak with concern) I fear they are almost the only
missionaries in America that do. My lord, I do not speak
rashly ; I have been in America, and so have several with
whom I have lately conversed, and both I and they know
what manner of men the greatest part of these are. They
are men who neither have the power of religion, nor the form ;
men that lay no claim to piety, nor even decency."

' (Smith's Methodism in Eastern British America.)

These are serious statements to be made by a clergyman
about fellow preachers in the same communion. Possibly
they did not apply to the eight of this denomination then in
Nova Scotia. But it is certain that after nine years of labor
along the Basin of Minas, Rev. Joseph Bennett, the resident
missionary, had but 48 communicants in a population of fully
a thousand Protestants.

The Presbyterianism of that day, moreover, lacked the life
and fervor which now give it such aggressive zeal. Most of
the New England settlers are said to have been Congregation-
alists, who had come out of the New England churches at a
time when the absence of religious earnestness in them is a
matter of well known history.

On every side, therefore, Alline found religious apathy,
indifference, and formality, where he looked for vital and
practical religion. Social services were rarely held. In 1782
one of the solid men of Liverpool, N. S., prominent in the
Congregational church there, wrote in his journal thus:
(Smith's Methodism in Eastern British America.)

" A religious meeting was held at my house in the evening ;
a large concourse of people, I believe nearly one hundred and
fifty, attended ; which is till of late a very strange thing in
this place, such a meeting having scarcely been known since
the settlement of it, till since Mr. Alline was here."

The disturbance of these cold and formal church relations
could not be an unmixed evil ; indeed, it was a necessary condition of genuine religious progress. Few men could have
done the work better than Alline. " To the one extreme of
cold religious doctrine he opposed the other extreme of feeling.
His religion was a religion of feeling. His writings glow
with it." The rapture he had felt when conscious of pardon
he assumed to be the test of religion in himself and others.
He appealed incessantly to the feelings of his hearers. " He
dwelt upon the greatness and glory of Christ, his compassion,
his humiliation, his bleeding love, his joy in saving sinners ;
or else mourning over the insensibility of those whom he ad-
dressed he sought to alarm them into feeling." He enforced
his teachings with affectionate earnestness, and throughout
all his toils and hardships displayed an elevated cheerfulness

and joy. He was a good singer, fervent in prayer, and pos-
sessed of a copious flow of language. This is evinced not
only by his printed sermons, but by the book of hymns which
he composed. Many of the young men who flocked to him
as leader, and who were converted and joined him in the
ministry, were of the same type. Passing from settlement to
settlement, " like religious knight-errants," they made, as was
natural, a profound impression. The slumbers of the churches
were thoroughly disturbed and the members were led to
active effort.

Alline's doctrinal views appear to have been fragmentary
and but slightly systematized. He saw in the plainest nar-
ratives and announcements of Scripture marvellous allegories.
He was indeed a mystic, but amid all his extravagances of
opinion his eminent and uniform piety showed that he " loved
God out of a pure heart fervently."

No distinct organization now exists as the result of the
work of Alline and his colleagues. The movement was an
offshoot of the great New Light movement which followed
the preaching of Whitefield in America, and in which Rhode
Island had no small share. Alline's followers were grouped
into churches resembling the Congregationalist bodies of
New England ; but little attention was paid to order or dis-
cipline, and as a consequence these organizations failed to be
permanent. In process of time the larger number of the
New Light preachers and their adherents, who had been
awakened under Alline's preaching and influence, became
Baptists and were gathered into churches of that faith and
order. A few became leaders among the Methodists. Certain it is that to the pioneer work of Alline and his fellow
laborers the Baptist denomination owes not only its numeri-
cal predominance in the fertile valleys of Nova Scotia, but

also the earnest, active type of practical religion which char-
acterizes it in that province. An appropriate gift, therefore,
was Henry Alline from the land of John Clarke and Roger
Williams to the colony at the north.

Of the descendants of the Rhode Island founders of Nova
Scotia, many have honorably distinguished themselves in
public and commercial life. The most eminent literary rep-
resentatives of the blood now living are doubtless Thomas B.
Akins, Record Commissioner at Halifax and editor of the
Archives of Nova Scotia, and Edward Young, LL. D., now
U, S. Consul at Windsor, N. S., but long connected with
the Treasury Department at Washington. Nicholas Mosher,
Esq., of Newport, was one of the pioneer ship-builders of
Nova Scotia, who represented his township in the Legislature,
and was a man of most extensive influence. The Northups
of Falmouth, have also been prominent. Jeremiah, the original settler, was the first member of the Provincial Assembly
from that township. His son John was for many years a
leading merchant of Halifax. A grandson of the latter, the
late Jeremiah Northup, was Senator of the Dominion of Canada for Nova Scotia. Edward Albro, Esq., is an aged and
prominent hardware merchant in Halifax. At Sackville, the
descendants of Valentine Esterbrooks have ever been numerous and influential; some thirty of the name are now upon
the voting list. A grandson of Eliphalet Reed still lives at
the age of ninety years and more, to encourage his two sons
in their work as Christian ministers. Dr. Edward A. Bowser,
the distinguised professor of mathematics at Rutgers College,
a native of Sackville, has a Rhode Island ancestry. It is now
evident, also, that we can add to this list the genial and witty
Thomas C. Haliburton who died in 1865, having been thirteen years a Judge in Nova Scotia and six years a Member
5

of Parliament in London, the author of "Sam Slick" and also of a "History of Nova Scotia." Thus Rhode Island can claim to have furnished the stock from which Canada has developed her finest literary flower.

In closing, let me allude to the interesting field opened by a knowledge of this emigration to our Rhode Island genealogists. The proprietors' records and probate records relating to the three townships of Falmouth, Newport, and Sackville, together with the lists of grantees and other lists of various periods found at Halifax, afford abundant ground for research respecting families and individuals who went thither. In some cases there is documentary evidence concerning Rhode Islanders who never left this colony. For example, on the Falmouth records I found an interesting page about a controversey relating to 43 acres of land in Charlestown, R. I., in which Capt. Edward York, of Falmouth, his wife Hannah, her father John Larkin, and her brother John Larkin, Jr. all figured. At Windsor I found a power of attorney signed by Christopher Allen of North Kingstown in 1761, and also the will of Edward Church of Little Compton, probated the same year. None of these, except Capt. York and his wife, were ever residents of Nova Scotia. Occasional references appear to the names of relatives in Rhode Island. I need not enlarge upon the value of such clues in the search for missing links.

I must, in a word more, allude to the aid rendered me in my hasty examination by several gentlemen and one lady upon the field. These are, in particular, Dr. David Allison and Mr. Thomas B. Akins of Halifax, Mr. C. W. Knowles and Dr. Edward Young of Windsor, Miss. Margaret Young of Falmouth, and Mr. William H. Knowles and Rev. John A. Mosher of Newport. These all, except Dr. Allison, share in a Rhode Island ancestry; and a l, without exception, merit the kindest thoughts of their kindred in Rhode Island for their generous service to a stranger, who bore no claim to their favor save his birth in the city of Roger Williams, and his deep interest in the land from which their fathers came.

APPENDIX.

I.

List of Persons to whom Town Lots were assigned at Falmouth Nov. 15, 1760. Taken from the Proprietors' Records. (It is possible that some of these names were added at a later date.)

Henry Dennie Denson	1	Joseph Wilson	14
"	2	Jabez Harrington	15
Henry Maturin Denson	3	Luke Horswell	16
Henry Maturin Denson ⎱	4	Joseph Steel	17
John Denson ⎰		Perry Borden	18
"	5	John Shaver	19
Timothy Saunders	6	Meeting Minister's Lot	20
Lucy Denson	7	Alex. McCullough	21
Nehemiah Wood	8	Adam McCullough	22
Edw. Ellis Watmouth	9	Ebenezer Millet	23
James H. Watmouth	10	George Lyde	24
Edmund Michenor	11	Thos. Akin	25
Michel Michenor ⎱	12	Moses Marsters ⎱	26
Matthew Michenor ⎰		Martha Dyer ⎰	
Abel Michenor	13	Edward York	27

Ichabod Stoddard	28	Benj. Gerrish, Esq.	61
" ⎱	29	Jonathan Davison	62
Wignul Cole ⎰		William Shey	63
"	30	Jona. Marsters	64
Thos. Woodworth	31	Jesse Crossman	65
Stephen Akin ⎱	32	Benj Salter	66
John Lovelass ⎰		John Meacham	67
John Steele	33	David Randall	68
John Hicks	34	Dan'l Hovey, Jr.	69
Abraham Wheeler	35	Eleazer Doane	70
Constant Church	36	Sam. Brow	71
Edward Church	37	William Wood ⎱	72
Terence Fitzpatrick	38	Peter Shaw ⎰	
Benoni Sweet ⎱	39	William Nevil Wolesley	73
Edw. Manchester ⎰		Abr. Marsters	74
Church of England Lot	40	Benj. Hicks	75
Walter Manning	41	Wm. Nevil Wolesley 1-2	76
John Gray	42	Fred'k. Delks Hore	77
Benj. Thurber	43	"	78
Chris. Dewey ⎱	44	Charles Proctor	79
Samuel Davison ⎰		John Hicks ⎱	80
John Davison	45	John Hicks Jr. ⎰	
William Allen	46	St. John Broderick	81
Mary Paysant	47	Samuel Broderick	82
James Wilson	48	Amos Wenman	83
Peter Shaw	49	William Shey	84
Condemned 50 to 54		Joseph Baley ⎱	85
Alex. Grant	55	Edward York ⎰	
Jere Northup	56	Dan'l Greeno	86
Joseph Northup	57	Benj. Gerrish	87
David Randall ⎱	58	Joseph Gooding	88
Cyprian Davison ⎰		Benj. Meyer	89
F. T. Muller	59	J. R. Muller	90
Joseph Jess	60	Shubael Dimock	91

John Simpson	92	William Church	100
Alex. Grant	93	Fork of River	
David Pake	94	Zach. Chase	1
Condemned	95	Nath. Reynolds	2
Abner Hall	96	Edw. Humblchatch	3
Barnabas Hall	97	Lieut. DesBarres	4
Abner Hall }	98	School Lot	5
Thomas Parker }		Henry Lyon	6
Amos Owen	99	John Almand	7

II.

Grantees of the Township of Newport, N. S., 1761, as entered upon the Proprietors' Records. Taken from an article in the Hants Journal contributed by Mr. Joseph Allison.

Joseph Bailey	Jonathan Babcock
Benjamin Sanford	Daniel Wier
Joshua Sanford	Jeremiah Baker
Benjamin Reynolds	Silas Weaver
Caleb Lake	James Card
James Mosher	Stephen Macumber
James Harvie	Levi Irish
John Woolhaber	Ichabod Macumber
Peter Shey	Cornelius Potter
Samuel Bentley	William Albro
James Smith	Samuel Brenton
James Simpson	Benjamin Wilcocks
Arnold Shaw	Michael Fish
Samuel Albro	John Wood

Joseph Sanford
Elisha Clark
John Slocum
Jonathan Rogers
John Gosbee
Zerobable Wastcoat
Robert Wastcoat
Benjamin Borden
Richard Card
James Weeden
Stephen Chapman
Gilbert Stuart
John Chambers
John Harvie
George Mumford
John Shaw
Edward Ellis
Encom Sanford
Joseph Straight
Henry Knowles
Robert Wastcoat Sr.
Stukely Wastcoat
John Jeffers

Daniel Dimock
James York
James Juhan
George Brightman
John Woodman
Joseph Wilson
Edward Church
Archibald Harvie
Samuel Borden
William Allen
William Hallyburton
Daniel Sanford
Aaron Butts
Moses De Les Dernier
Gideon De Les Dernier
Peter Bourgeois
Jonathan Card
Abel Michener
James Harvie Jr.
Isaac Deschamps
Benjamin Walley
Amos Walley

III.

" The List of the Subscribers for the Township Lying on Tantimar River, Represented by Benjamin Thurber. Cyprian Sterry and Edmund Jinks. from Providence in Rhodisland." Taken from records in the Province Library at Halifax. The date is probably 1761, but possibly 1760.

Jos. Olney
John Jenckes
Solo. Wheat
Benj'n Thurber
Cyprian Sterry
Edmund Jenckes
David Burr
Jos. Tower
Seth Luther
Jno. Young
Sam Thurber
Jacob Whitman
Edmund Tripp
David Waters
William Sheldon
Dan'l Wear
Rich'd Brown
Volintine Easterbrooks
Charles Olney
Thos. Field
Thos. Bowen
Jona. Jenckes
Step. Jenckes
James Olney
Wm. Brown
Sam'l Lethredge
Gershom Holden
Sam'l Currey
John Foster
Sam'l Clark
Nathan Case
Eben'r Robins

Wm. Clark
Jona. Olney
Wm. Ford
Sam'l Wetherby
Step. Angel
Peleg Williams
Jona. Allen
Peter Randal
John Tripp
Nath Day
John Malavery
Noah Whitman
Nath Bucklin
Noah Mason
Rob't Sterry

The above
mentioned names for
One share and a half.

47
23 1-2
———
70 1-2

Elisha Hopkins
Wm. Walcot
David Alberson
Rob't Potter
Dan'l Wilcocks
John Mullin
Robt Woodward
Peter Bateman

Daniel Thurber
Daniel Cahoon
Chas. Symons
Benj. Gorman
John Howland
Nathan Jenckes
David Tift
Jos. Brown
Gideon Smith
Jos. Hawkins
Sarah Cottle
Isaac Cole
Obediah King
Thos. Woodward
Rob't Foster
Jer. Brownel
Nath'l Finney
John Dexter
Steph. Carpenter
Levi Potter
Nedebiah Angel
John Brown
James Foster
Sam'l Briggs
James Young
Ichabod Cumstock
Morris Hern
Jos. Burden
Ezra Heyley
Obediah Sprauge (sic)
Edward Thurber
John Olney

Sam'l Toogood
Jos. Olney, Jr.
Wm. Whipple
David Wilbur
Oliver Casey
Elisha Smith
Nathan Case Jr.
Charles Angel
Jos. Taylor
Oliver Man
Moses Man
W. Whipple, Jr.
Wm. Phillips
Benj. Robinson
Jona. Pike
George Wear
Edward Giles
John Smith
Gilbert Samons
Woodbery Morris
John Wiever
Nehemiah Sweet
Stephen Goodspeed
Abraham Olney
James Muzey
Jeremiah Dexter
William Jenckes
Henry Finch
Sam'l Shearman
Wm. Olney
John Olney Jr.
James Olney

William Olney, Jr.

Coggeshal Olney

John Power

Aaron Mason

Nathan Jenckes

Freelove Tucker

Benja. Cousins

Rowland Sprague

Nathan Giles

Benja. Medberry

Nathanael Woodward

Zeph'r Woodward

James Jenckes

William Emerson

Chas. Spaulding

John Downer

Nath'l Packer

Thos Sterry

Amasa Kilburn

Nathan Sterry

Samuel Mott

James Day of Massachusetts.

Asa Foster   "

John Peabody   "

Peter Parker,   "

Isaac Blunt,   "

Caleby Swan,   "

Francis Swan, of Massachus's

Daniel Ingols,   "

John Wilson, .   "

Nath'l Brown,   "

Abiel Fry,   "

Simon Fry,   "

Bemsley Stevens,   "

Rob't Davis,   "

Jer. Dexter (erased)

These single
shares each
154
47
———
107
70 1-2
———
177 1-2

45 first settlers
66   2   do.
66   3   do.
———
177

On the back of the paper is written:
" List of Tantamar Proprietors,"
        also
" A List of the Settlers from Providence in Rhode Island
Colony."

IV.

" Return of the State of the Township of Falmouth, Jan, 1, 1770." Taken from records in the Province Library at Halifax. The names alone are here given ; but the original states the number in each family and classifies the property of each.

Henry Denny Denson
Abel Michenor
Joseph Wilson
Joseph Jess
Levi Irish
Ichabod Stoddard
Edward Yorke
Wignall Cole
Thomas Woodworth
Stephen Aken
John Potter
Constant Church
John Simpson
Jonathan Vickery
Tamerlain Campbell
George Stuart
Christopher Knight
Peter Manning

John Davison
William Allen
Malachy Cagan
Edward Manchester
Jeremia Northup
Jacob Mullar
William Shey
Benjamin Gerrish
Jonathan Marsters
John Loveless
I. F. W. DesBarres
George Faesch
Henry Lyon
James Wilson
Luke Horswell *
Timothy Davison
Terence Fitzpatrick

(* The record states that this man and his family had left the province within a year.)

V.

Return of the State of the Township of Sackville, Jan. 1, 1770. Taken from the records in the Province Library, Halifax.

Sam'l Bellew
John Peck
Joseph Collins
Gideon Young
Sam'l Rogers
Joshua Sprague
John Olney
William Lawrance
Robert Foster
James Jinks
John Barnes
Jacob Bacon
George Shearman
Nath'l Finney
William Olney
William Alverson
Ezekiel Fuller
Jeremiah Brownell
Daniel Hawkins
David Tift
Ameriah Telland
Thomas Irons
Thomas Collins
Nathan'l Rounds
Amasa Kellum
Robert Scott
Calyb Finney
Stephen Johnson
Samuel Lettimore
Gideon Smith
George Shearman, Jr.
Nathan Mason
Nathaniel Mason

Nathan Simmons
Samuel Emerson
David Alverson
Benjamin Tower
Joseph Tower
John Day
Valentine Esterbrooks
Robert Lettimore
Eliphalet Reed
Seth Hervey
Gilbert Simmons
Jacob Fuller
Josiah Tingley
Benajah Lewis
John Thomas
Job Simmons
Epherim Emerson
Benja. Emerson
Ebenezer Salisbury
Eben Salisbury, Jr.
Isreal Thornton
Isaiah Horton
Nehemiah Ward
Jonathan Cole
William Baker
Joseph Baker
William Simmons
Benja. Mason
Samuel Lewis
Samuel Eddy
John Wood
Sam'l Irons

VI.

Roll or Inventory of Estates in the Township of Newport, Dec. 30, 1772. Taken from records in the Province Library, Halifax. The date and some of the names are almost illegible.

Encom Sanford
George Brightman
James Smith
Joseph Bailey, Esq.
Henry Knowles
John Smith, Canetcook.
John Lawrillard
Benja. Wier
John M . . . . . .
Thomas Baker
William Reed }
William Sterling }
Thomas Allen
William Coffell
Isaac Deschamps, Esq.
Barzilhai Mosher
Francis Smith
Samuel Cottnam
Archibald Harvie
John Brown
James Simpson
   (agent for Tucker)
Ichabod Macomber
Daniel Dimock
Abraham Ada . . . . .
Robert Waistoc
James Dormond

Sam'l Bentley
John Wood
Woodward Sanford
James Card
Jeremiah Baker
Thom. Cochran
John Simson
Robert Scott
Daniel Wiever
Stephen Wilcox
James Campbell
John Anthony
James Harvie, Jr.
Benjamin Burges
George Sharahe
James Fish
Michael Fish,
   widow her share
Daniel Greeno
James Simpson
John Harvie
John Mosher
William Bentley
James Harvie
John Chambers
Shubael Dimock
Amos Walley

Stephen Macomber
William Smith
Hugh Smith
Benja. Sanford
John Canavan
John Dinsmore
James Mosher
William Smith, Irish
William Wier
William Wier for Mr, Shay
Caleb Lake
. . . . . Sanford
George Mumford

James Harvie. Jr. & }
Stephen Wilcocks }
Benja. Wilcocks
Robert Salter
Archibald Harvie
John Woodman
John Carder
Phillip Mosher
Job Card
James Dormond
Cornelius Potter
Abel Michenor

VII.

" A list of persons in Newport Township, Nova Scotia, qualified to serve on Juries," 1781. Taken from the papers of Isaac Deschamps by Thomas B. Akins, Esq.

James Camble
James Mosher
Allen Mosher
John Cannan
Hugh Smith
Wm. Smith
. . . . hen Macomber
Amos Waley
Acey Limock
Thomas Baker
John Marsters

Dan'l Dimick
John Lawald
Ichabod McComber
Stephen Macoomber
John Almand
James Fogson
. . . . . Mosher
John Bentley
Barsiler Mosher
Jonathan Knowles
John Smith

John Chambers
James Ballor
Wm. MacCoy
Shub'l Dimock
. . . . . McComber
. . . . . Pawper
. . . . ham Reid
Francis Mason
Dan'l Weden
Wm. Weden
Philip Mosher
Edw'd Mosher
John Macnutt
Beniamen Wier
John Brown
Joseph Baley
Archibald Harvey
Francis Smith
Wm. Smith
John Roug

Jas. Fish
Daniel Greno
Geo. Sharon
John Harvie
Wm. Coffin
Jas. Simpson
Thos. Smith
Particat Casey
Arnold Shaw
Juda Shaw
John Wier
James Dearmet
Sam'l Donsmore
Jas. Donsmore
Francis Donsmore
Francis Parker
Ezek'l Marsters
Wm. Sterling
Beniamen Sweet

Sept. 5, 1781.   E. Mosher, Constable.

This is a list of all th . . . . . this side of Cannetcut River.

Wm. Smith
John Anthony
David Anthony
Noah Anthony
John Smith
James Wier
Wm Wier

Caleb Lake
Will'm Lake
. . . . . Britman
. . . . . Sandford
Benjamen Wilcocks
Stephen Wilcocks
Rob't Wilcocks

Woodward Sanford

Osborn Sanford

Peleg Sanford

James Harvie

Rob't Salter

Will'm Salter

John Burges

Edward Burges

Cornelius Potter

Stephen Potter

John Card

Job Card

Thomas Allen

William Albro

VIII.

Notes relating to the Rhode Island Settlers at Newport and Falmouth, N. S., taken from the offices of the Register of Deeds and the Register of Probate, at Windsor, N. S.

Transfers of Real Estate.

1. Christopher Allen of North Kingstown, R. I., to Stukeley Wascoat of Newport, N. S.; power of attorney relating to draught of lands; June 23, 1761.

2. James Mosher, attorney for Aaron Butts, to John Chambers; Apr. 14, 1763.

3. John Jeffers, lease to John Harvie and John Chambers; Apr. 15, 1763.

4. Joseph Straight to John Chambers; Apr. 14, 1763.

5. John Steele to Moses Deles Dernier, Nov. 9, 1763.

6. Benjamin Borden to Benjamin Sanford, Dec. 13, 1763.

7. James Mosher to James Simpson, Mar. 2, 1762. Encom Sanford, witness.

8.   Joshua Sanford to James Simpson, Feb. 6, 1762.

9.   Jonathan Babcock to James Simpson, Oct. 25, 1762.

10.   James Weeden to James Card, Sept. 30, 1762. Silas Wever, witness.

11.   Sam'l Bentley to . . . . June 1, 1762.

12.   Nehemiah Wood to . . . . Mar. 1, 1763.

13.   Benjamin Reynolds to Stephen Macomber, May 12, 1764.

14.   William Albro to James Smith, Apr. 14, 1763.

15.   Zerobbabel Wastcoat to John Chambers and James Smith, 1763. (Probably Apr. 14.)

16.   John Woodman to John Chambers, Apr. 14, 1763.

17.   Sam'l Brown, brickmaker, to Sam'l Watts, tavern-keeper, Falmouth.

18.   Eben'r Millett to Thomas Woodworth, Sept. 8, 1764.

Wills.

[Dat. – dated; p. – admitted to probate.]

1.   Edward Church of Little Compton, dat. Aug. 15, 1757, p. Sept. 17, 1761; mentions son Constant.

2.   Stephen Chapman, Newport, N. S.; dat. 3d. mo., 12, 1765; mentions wife Zeruiah, children Nathaniel, Rufus, William, Dorcas, Lucy.

3.   James Wilson, Falmouth; mentions brother William Wilson, sister Ruth Wilson, cousin Barnabas Wilson.

4.   Richard Card, dat. Sept. 28, 1773, p. Sept. 18, 1775.

5. James Card, dat. Jan. 13, 1778, p. Mar. 28, 1778.

6. James Weeden. dat. May 27, 1777, p. Dec. 29, 1783; mentions wife Mary, children Daniel, Naomi Weeden, William, Mary Canavan.

7. George Brightman, dat. Jan. 5, 1786, p. May 1, 1786; mentions honored father, children (under age) George, Susannah, Lydia, Mary, Elizabeth, Esther and Hannah, his nephew George Dimock, and his brother Thomas Brightman.

8. Joseph Bailey, dat. Apr. 7, 1787, p. Aug. 27. 1787; mentions son Joseph Sanford Bailey, daughters Deborah Dimock and Sarah Brown, grandchildren (the above mentioned children of George Brightman) and his wife Hannah.

9. James Harvey, dat. June 26, 1786, p. Dec. 19, 1792; mentions sons John, Archibald and James, and daughter Margaret.

10. Wignal Cole, dat. Mar. 27, 1789, p. May 23, 1794; mentions sister Susannah Cole in Rhode Island, and William Cole, son of eldest brother John, in Rhode Island.

11. Benjamin Wilcox, Mar. 3, 1813, mentions eldest son Stephen, sons Robert and Gardiner, daughters Else Harvey, Hittabel Sanford, Francis Card, Esther Mosher, Susannah Lake, Hannah Brown, Mary Armstrong, and his granddaughter Esther.

12. Henry Knowles; inventory Jan. 20, 1800, mentions daughter Martha sixteen years old, his mother, and his wife Molly. Receipts are signed by William Knowles, Sabray Knowles, Nathan Knowles, ... (possibly Catharine) Knowles, Joshua Smith, Sarah Smith, Molly Knowles and Martha Knowles.   7